50 The Best Japanese Dessert Recipes

By: Kelly Johnson

Table of Contents

- Mochi
- Daifuku (stuffed mochi)
- Warabi Mochi
- Matcha Ice Cream
- Hojicha Ice Cream
- Shiratama Dango
- Mitarashi Dango
- Anmitsu
- Dorayaki
- Taiyaki
- Imagawayaki
- Yatsuhashi
- Yokan
- Uiro
- Kuzumochi
- Castella Cake
- Japanese Cheesecake
- Matcha Basque Cheesecake
- Japanese Soufflé Pancakes
- Purin (Japanese Custard Pudding)
- Coffee Jelly
- Anpan (Sweet Red Bean Bun)
- Melonpan
- Cream Pan
- Matcha Tiramisu
- Matcha Roll Cake
- Strawberry Shortcake
- Baumkuchen
- Hojicha Pudding
- Mochi Ice Cream
- Kinako Mochi
- Sakuramochi
- Kusa Mochi
- Monaka
- Nama Chocolate
- Chinsuko (Okinawan Shortbread Cookies)

- Sata Andagi (Okinawan Doughnuts)
- Zenzai (Sweet Red Bean Soup)
- Kabocha Purin
- Matcha Chiffon Cake
- Japanese Fruit Sandwich
- Mizu Yokan
- Hanami Dango
- Hishi Mochi
- Nerikiri Wagashi
- Suama
- Karinto
- Higashi
- Baked Sweet Potato (Yaki Imo)
- Japanese Parfait

Homemade Mochi

Ingredients:

- 1 cup **glutinous rice flour** (Mochiko)
- 3/4 cup **water**
- 1/4 cup **sugar**
- 1/2 teaspoon **vanilla extract** (optional)
- **Cornstarch or potato starch** (for dusting)

Optional Fillings:

- Sweet red bean paste
- Ice cream
- Nutella

Instructions:

1. Prepare the Dough:

1. In a microwave-safe bowl, mix **glutinous rice flour**, **sugar**, and **water** until smooth.
2. Cover loosely with plastic wrap.

2. Cook the Mochi:

Microwave Method:

- Microwave for 1 minute, stir, then microwave for another 1 minute. Stir again.
- Microwave for 30 more seconds or until the mixture becomes thick and sticky.

Stovetop Method:

- Pour the mixture into a heatproof bowl and place it in a steamer.
- Steam for about **15 minutes**, stirring occasionally.

3. Shape the Mochi:

1. Dust a clean surface with **cornstarch or potato starch**.
2. Transfer the hot mochi dough onto the dusted surface.
3. Let it cool slightly, then dust your hands with starch and knead gently.
4. Roll the mochi into a **flat sheet** (about 1/4 inch thick).

4. Fill and Shape (Optional):

- If using a **filling**, cut the mochi into small circles.
- Place a small amount of **red bean paste, ice cream, or Nutella** in the center.
- Pinch the edges together to seal and form a ball.

5. Serve:

- Enjoy immediately or store in an airtight container at room temperature for a day.

Daifuku (Stuffed Mochi)

Ingredients:

- 1 cup **glutinous rice flour** (Mochiko)
- 3/4 cup **water**
- 1/4 cup **sugar**
- **Cornstarch or potato starch** (for dusting)
- **Filling options:** sweet red bean paste, Nutella, ice cream, strawberries

Instructions:

1. Mix **glutinous rice flour, sugar, and water** until smooth.
2. Microwave for 1 minute, stir, then microwave for another 1 minute. Stir again.
3. Microwave for 30 more seconds or steam for 15 minutes until thick.
4. Dust a surface with starch, transfer mochi, and roll out.
5. Cut into small circles, place filling in the center, and pinch to seal.
6. Serve immediately or store in an airtight container.

Warabi Mochi

Ingredients:

- 1/2 cup **warabiko (bracken starch)**
- 2 cups **water**
- 1/4 cup **sugar**
- **Kinako (roasted soybean flour) for dusting**
- **Kuromitsu (brown sugar syrup) for drizzling**

Instructions:

1. Mix **warabiko, sugar, and water** in a saucepan over medium heat.
2. Stir continuously until thick and translucent.
3. Transfer to a starch-dusted surface, let cool, and cut into bite-sized pieces.
4. Dust with kinako and drizzle with kuromitsu before serving.

Matcha Ice Cream

Ingredients:

- 2 cups **heavy cream**
- 1 cup **whole milk**
- 3 tbsp **matcha powder**
- 3/4 cup **sugar**
- 4 **egg yolks**
- 1 tsp **vanilla extract**

Instructions:

1. Whisk **matcha powder and milk** until dissolved.
2. Heat **milk mixture and half the sugar** until warm.
3. Whisk **egg yolks and remaining sugar**, then slowly add warm milk while whisking.
4. Cook over low heat until thickened.
5. Strain, mix with heavy cream and vanilla, then chill.
6. Churn in an ice cream maker and freeze until firm.

Hojicha Ice Cream

Ingredients:

- 2 cups **heavy cream**
- 1 cup **whole milk**
- 3 tbsp **hojicha tea leaves**
- 3/4 cup **sugar**
- 4 **egg yolks**
- 1 tsp **vanilla extract**

Instructions:

1. Heat **milk and hojicha tea leaves**, then steep for 10 minutes. Strain.
2. Add **half the sugar** and warm the mixture.
3. Whisk **egg yolks and remaining sugar**, then slowly add the warm milk while whisking.
4. Cook over low heat until thickened.
5. Strain, mix with heavy cream and vanilla, then chill.
6. Churn in an ice cream maker and freeze until firm.

Shiratama Dango

Ingredients:

- 1 cup **shiratamako (glutinous rice flour)**
- 1/2 cup **water**
- **Kinako (roasted soybean flour) or sweet red bean paste** for topping

Instructions:

1. Gradually mix water into shiratamako until dough forms.
2. Roll into small balls and boil until they float (about 2-3 minutes).
3. Transfer to ice water, then drain.
4. Serve with kinako, red bean paste, or syrup.

Mitarashi Dango

Ingredients:

- 1 cup **shiratamako**
- 1/2 cup **water**
- **Sauce:** 3 tbsp **soy sauce**, 3 tbsp **sugar**, 2 tbsp **mirin**, 1 tsp **potato starch + 1 tbsp water**

Instructions:

1. Prepare and boil dango as above, then skewer.
2. Simmer soy sauce, sugar, and mirin, then add starch slurry to thicken.
3. Brush sauce onto dango and lightly grill or serve as is.

Anmitsu

Ingredients:

- 1/2 cup **kanten (agar) powder**
- 2 cups **water**
- 2 tbsp **sugar**
- **Toppings:** sweet red bean paste, fruit, mochi, ice cream
- **Kuromitsu syrup:** 3 tbsp **brown sugar**, 2 tbsp **water**

Instructions:

1. Dissolve kanten in boiling water, then add sugar and cool until set.
2. Cut into cubes and serve with toppings and kuromitsu drizzle.

Dorayaki

Ingredients:

- 1 cup **flour**
- 2 **eggs**
- 1/2 cup **sugar**
- 1/2 tsp **baking soda**
- 1 tbsp **honey**
- 1/3 cup **water**
- **Filling:** sweet red bean paste

Instructions:

1. Whisk eggs, sugar, honey, and water. Sift in flour and baking soda.
2. Cook small pancakes in a greased pan.
3. Sandwich red bean paste between two pancakes.

Taiyaki

Ingredients:

- 1 cup **flour**
- 1/2 tsp **baking powder**
- 1 tbsp **sugar**
- 1/2 cup **water or milk**
- 1 **egg**
- **Filling:** red bean paste, custard, chocolate

Instructions:

1. Mix batter and let rest for 10 minutes.
2. Pour into a taiyaki mold, add filling, then cover with more batter.
3. Cook until golden on both sides.

Imagawayaki

Ingredients:

- 1 cup **flour**
- 1/2 tsp **baking powder**
- 2 tbsp **sugar**
- 1/2 cup **milk**
- 1 **egg**
- **Filling:** red bean paste, custard

Instructions:

1. Prepare batter and let it rest.
2. Pour into a round mold or pan, add filling, and cover with more batter.
3. Cook until golden on both sides.

Yatsuhashi

Ingredients:

- 1/2 cup **glutinous rice flour**
- 1/4 cup **sugar**
- 1/2 cup **water**
- 1/2 tsp **cinnamon**
- **Filling:** sweet red bean paste (optional)

Instructions:

1. Mix rice flour, sugar, water, and cinnamon. Steam for 15 minutes.
2. Roll out, cut into squares, and fold over red bean paste if filling.

Yokan

Ingredients:

- 1/2 cup **red bean paste**
- 1 tsp **agar powder**
- 1 cup **water**
- 2 tbsp **sugar**

Instructions:

1. Dissolve agar in boiling water, then add sugar and red bean paste.
2. Stir until thick, pour into a mold, and cool until firm.

Uiro

Ingredients:

- 1 cup **rice flour**
- 1/2 cup **sugar**
- 1 cup **water**

Instructions:

1. Mix all ingredients and pour into a heatproof dish.
2. Steam for 30 minutes, then cool and slice.

Kuzumochi

Ingredients:

- 1/2 cup **kudzu starch**
- 1 1/2 cups **water**
- 1/4 cup **sugar**
- **Toppings:** kinako, kuromitsu

Instructions:

1. Mix kudzu starch, sugar, and water in a saucepan over low heat.
2. Stir continuously until thick and transparent.
3. Pour into a mold, cool, and cut into squares.

Castella Cake

Ingredients:

- 4 **eggs**
- 1 cup **sugar**
- 1 cup **bread flour**
- 2 tbsp **honey**
- 2 tbsp **warm water**

Instructions:

1. Beat eggs and sugar until fluffy.
2. Mix in honey and warm water, then sift in flour.
3. Bake at 325°F (160°C) for 40 minutes.

Japanese Cheesecake

Ingredients:

- 1 package **cream cheese**
- 1/2 cup **sugar**
- 3 **eggs**
- 1/2 cup **milk**
- 1/2 cup **cake flour**
- 1 tbsp **lemon juice**
- 1/4 tsp **cream of tartar**

Instructions:

1. Preheat the oven to 320°F (160°C).
2. Beat cream cheese and sugar until smooth.
3. Add eggs one at a time, then mix in milk, flour, and lemon juice.
4. Fold in stiffly beaten egg whites with cream of tartar.
5. Pour into a greased pan and bake in a water bath for 50 minutes.
6. Cool and refrigerate before serving.

Matcha Basque Cheesecake

Ingredients:

- 1 package **cream cheese**
- 1/2 cup **sugar**
- 2 **eggs**
- 1 tbsp **matcha powder**
- 1/2 cup **heavy cream**
- 1/4 cup **flour**

Instructions:

1. Preheat the oven to 400°F (200°C).
2. Beat cream cheese and sugar, then add eggs and heavy cream.
3. Sift in matcha powder and flour, mixing until smooth.
4. Pour into a greased, parchment-lined pan and bake for 25 minutes.
5. Let cool before serving.

Japanese Soufflé Pancakes

Ingredients:

- 1/2 cup **flour**
- 2 **egg yolks**
- 2 **egg whites**
- 1/4 cup **milk**
- 2 tbsp **sugar**
- 1/2 tsp **baking powder**
- **Butter for cooking**

Instructions:

1. Mix egg yolks, milk, sugar, and flour into a smooth batter.
2. Beat egg whites to stiff peaks and fold into the batter.
3. Grease a pan and cook pancakes on low heat, covering with a lid.
4. Flip carefully and cook until golden brown.
5. Serve with syrup, whipped cream, or fresh fruits.

Purin (Japanese Custard Pudding)

Ingredients:

- 1 cup **milk**
- 2 **eggs**
- 1/4 cup **sugar**
- 1 tsp **vanilla extract**
- **Caramel**: 1/4 cup **sugar**, 1 tbsp **water**

Instructions:

1. Heat sugar and water in a pan to make caramel, then pour into ramekins.
2. Mix eggs, sugar, milk, and vanilla, then strain.
3. Pour over caramel and steam for 20 minutes or bake in a water bath for 40 minutes.
4. Let cool and refrigerate.

Coffee Jelly

Ingredients:

- 2 cups **strong coffee**
- 2 tbsp **sugar**
- 2 tsp **gelatin powder**

Instructions:

1. Dissolve sugar in hot coffee.
2. Sprinkle gelatin into the coffee, then stir until dissolved.
3. Pour into molds and chill for 3–4 hours.
4. Serve with whipped cream or condensed milk.

Anpan (Sweet Red Bean Bun)

Ingredients:

- 1 1/4 cups **bread flour**
- 1/4 cup **sugar**
- 1/2 tsp **salt**
- 1/2 tsp **instant yeast**
- 1/2 cup **milk**
- 1/4 cup **butter**
- 1/2 cup **anko (sweet red bean paste)**

Instructions:

1. Mix flour, sugar, salt, yeast, and warm milk, then knead until smooth.
2. Let dough rise for an hour.
3. Divide dough, wrap in red bean paste, and shape into buns.
4. Let rise again, then bake at 350°F (175°C) for 15 minutes.

Melonpan (Japanese Melon Bread)

Ingredients:

- 2 cups **bread flour**
- 1/2 cup **sugar**
- 1 tsp **instant yeast**
- 1/4 cup **milk**
- 1/4 cup **butter**
- 1 **egg**
- **Cookie dough topping**: 1/2 cup **flour**, 1/4 cup **sugar**, 1/4 cup **butter**, 1 egg yolk, a few drops of **vanilla**

Instructions:

1. Mix flour, sugar, yeast, milk, butter, and egg to form dough, then let rise.
2. Prepare cookie dough by combining ingredients and rolling out into thin sheets.
3. Wrap cookie dough around risen dough balls.
4. Bake at 350°F (175°C) for 15–20 minutes.

Cream Pan (Cream-filled Bread)

Ingredients:

- 2 cups **bread flour**
- 1/4 cup **sugar**
- 1 tsp **instant yeast**
- 1/2 cup **milk**
- 1/4 cup **butter**
- **Custard cream**: 1/2 cup **milk**, 2 **egg yolks**, 2 tbsp **sugar**, 1 tbsp **cornstarch**

Instructions:

1. Prepare dough by mixing bread flour, sugar, yeast, milk, and butter, then let rise.
2. Make custard cream by heating milk and whisking with sugar, egg yolks, and cornstarch until thickened.
3. Divide dough, fill with custard, and shape into rolls.
4. Bake at 350°F (175°C) for 15 minutes.

Matcha Tiramisu

Ingredients:

- 1/2 cup **heavy cream**
- 1/4 cup **sugar**
- 1 cup **mascarpone cheese**
- 1 tbsp **matcha powder**
- 1 cup **strong green tea**
- **Ladyfingers**

Instructions:

1. Whip cream and sugar until soft peaks form, then fold in mascarpone.
2. Mix matcha powder with green tea.
3. Dip ladyfingers into matcha tea, layer in a dish, and top with mascarpone mixture.
4. Repeat layers and refrigerate for 4 hours.

Matcha Roll Cake

Ingredients:

- 3 **eggs**
- 1/4 cup **sugar**
- 1/2 cup **cake flour**
- 1 tbsp **matcha powder**
- 1/4 cup **milk**
- 1/4 cup **butter**

Instructions:

1. Beat eggs with sugar until light and fluffy.
2. Sift in cake flour and matcha, then fold in milk and melted butter.
3. Bake at 350°F (175°C) for 12–15 minutes.
4. Roll with whipped cream and matcha filling.

Strawberry Shortcake

Ingredients:

- 1 cup **flour**
- 1/4 cup **sugar**
- 1/4 cup **milk**
- 1/2 cup **heavy cream**
- 1 tsp **baking powder**
- **Strawberries, sliced**
- **Whipped cream**

Instructions:

1. Mix flour, sugar, baking powder, milk, and cream, then bake at 350°F (175°C) for 25 minutes.
2. Cool, then slice and layer with strawberries and whipped cream.

Baumkuchen

Ingredients:

- 4 **eggs**
- 1/2 cup **sugar**
- 1/2 cup **honey**
- 1/2 cup **milk**
- 1 cup **cake flour**
- 1/2 tsp **baking powder**
- 2 tbsp **melted butter**

Instructions:

1. Beat eggs and sugar until fluffy.
2. Mix in honey, milk, flour, and baking powder.
3. Cook in thin layers in a round pan, brushing with butter between each layer.
4. Continue layering and baking until golden.

Hojicha Pudding

Ingredients:

- 1 cup **milk**
- 1 tbsp **hojicha tea leaves**
- 2 tbsp **sugar**
- 1 tsp **gelatin + 1 tbsp water**

Instructions:

1. Heat milk with hojicha leaves and sugar, then strain.
2. Dissolve gelatin in water and mix into the milk.
3. Pour into molds and chill for 2 hours.

Mochi Ice Cream

Ingredients:

- 1 cup **shiratamako (glutinous rice flour)**
- 1/4 cup **sugar**
- 3/4 cup **water**
- **Ice cream scoops**
- **Cornstarch for dusting**

Instructions:

1. Mix shiratamako, sugar, and water, then microwave for 2 minutes.
2. Stir, then microwave for another 30 seconds.
3. Roll out, cut circles, and wrap around ice cream scoops.
4. Freeze until firm.

Kinako Mochi

Ingredients:

- 1 cup **shiratamako**
- 3/4 cup **water**
- 1/4 cup **sugar**
- **Kinako (roasted soybean flour) + sugar for coating**

Instructions:

1. Mix shiratamako, sugar, and water, then steam for 15 minutes.
2. Knead until smooth, cut into pieces, and coat with kinako.

Sakuramochi

Ingredients:

- 1 cup **shiratamako**
- 3/4 cup **water**
- 1/4 cup **sugar**
- **Sweet red bean paste**
- **Salted cherry leaves**

Instructions:

1. Mix shiratamako, sugar, and water, then steam for 15 minutes.
2. Wrap mochi around red bean paste and cover with cherry leaves.

Kusa Mochi

Ingredients:

- 1 cup **shiratamako**
- 1/2 cup **yomogi (mugwort) paste**
- 3/4 cup **water**
- 1/4 cup **sugar**

Instructions:

1. Mix shiratamako, sugar, and water, then steam for 15 minutes.
2. Knead in yomogi paste, then shape into pieces.

Monaka

Ingredients:

- **Monaka wafers** (store-bought or homemade)
- **Sweet red bean paste**

Instructions:

1. Spoon red bean paste onto a monaka wafer.
2. Press another wafer on top and serve.

Nama Chocolate

Ingredients:

- 200g **dark chocolate**
- 100ml **heavy cream**
- 1 tbsp **butter**
- **Cocoa powder for dusting**

Instructions:

1. Heat cream and butter, then mix with chopped chocolate until smooth.
2. Pour into a lined tray, chill, and cut into squares.
3. Dust with cocoa powder before serving.

Chinsuko (Okinawan Shortbread Cookies)

Ingredients:

- 1 cup **flour**
- 1/4 cup **sugar**
- 1/4 cup **lard or butter**

Instructions:

1. Mix flour, sugar, and lard until dough forms.
2. Shape into small cookies and bake at 320°F (160°C) for 15 minutes.

Sata Andagi (Okinawan Doughnuts)

Ingredients:

- 2 cups **flour**
- 1/2 cup **sugar**
- 1 tsp **baking powder**
- 2 **eggs**
- 2 tbsp **milk**
- **Oil for frying**

Instructions:

1. Mix all ingredients into a thick dough.
2. Roll into balls and deep-fry until golden.

Zenzai (Sweet Red Bean Soup)

Ingredients:

- 1 cup **azuki beans**
- 4 cups **water**
- 1/2 cup **sugar**
- **Mochi pieces**

Instructions:

1. Simmer azuki beans in water for 1 hour until soft.
2. Add sugar and simmer until thickened.
3. Serve with toasted mochi pieces.

Kabocha Purin (Pumpkin Custard Pudding)

Ingredients:

- 1/2 cup **kabocha pumpkin (steamed and mashed)**
- 1 cup **milk**
- 2 **eggs**
- 1/4 cup **sugar**
- 1 tsp **vanilla extract**
- **Caramel:** 1/4 cup **sugar**, 1 tbsp **water**

Instructions:

1. Heat sugar and water in a pan until golden, then pour into ramekins.
2. Blend kabocha, milk, eggs, sugar, and vanilla until smooth.
3. Strain and pour over caramel.
4. Steam for 20 minutes or bake in a water bath at 300°F (150°C) for 40 minutes.

Matcha Chiffon Cake

Ingredients:

- 4 **eggs (separated)**
- 3/4 cup **cake flour**
- 1 tbsp **matcha powder**
- 1/2 cup **sugar**
- 1/4 cup **milk**
- 1/4 cup **vegetable oil**
- 1/2 tsp **baking powder**

Instructions:

1. Whisk egg yolks, oil, and milk.
2. Sift in flour, matcha, and baking powder.
3. Beat egg whites with sugar until stiff peaks form, then fold into batter.
4. Pour into an ungreased chiffon cake pan and bake at 325°F (160°C) for 40 minutes.

Japanese Fruit Sandwich

Ingredients:

- 4 slices **shokupan (Japanese milk bread)**
- 1/2 cup **heavy cream**
- 1 tbsp **sugar**
- **Fresh fruit (strawberries, kiwi, mango, etc.)**

Instructions:

1. Whip cream and sugar until soft peaks form.
2. Spread whipped cream on bread slices.
3. Arrange fruit and cover with another layer of cream.
4. Place another slice of bread on top, wrap, and chill before slicing.

Mizu Yokan (Chilled Red Bean Jelly)

Ingredients:

- 1 cup **anko (sweet red bean paste)**
- 1 1/4 cups **water**
- 1 tsp **agar-agar powder**

Instructions:

1. Heat water and agar until dissolved.
2. Mix in anko and stir until smooth.
3. Pour into a mold and chill until firm.

Hanami Dango (Three-Color Skewered Mochi)

Ingredients:

- 1 cup **shiratamako (glutinous rice flour)**
- 3/4 cup **water**
- 1/4 cup **sugar**
- **Pink food coloring & matcha powder**

Instructions:

1. Mix shiratamako, sugar, and water, then divide into three portions.
2. Dye one portion pink, leave one white, and mix matcha into the last one.
3. Boil the dango balls until they float, then cool in ice water.
4. Skewer one of each color onto bamboo sticks.

Hishi Mochi (Layered Diamond Mochi)

Ingredients:

- 1 cup **shiratamako (glutinous rice flour)**
- 3/4 cup **water**
- 1/4 cup **sugar**
- **Pink food coloring & matcha powder**

Instructions:

1. Divide shiratamako, sugar, and water into three bowls.
2. Dye one portion pink, mix matcha into another, and leave one white.
3. Steam each layer separately, then press them into a mold in the order: pink, white, green.
4. Cool, then cut into diamond shapes.

Nerikiri Wagashi (Sweet Bean Paste Confections)

Ingredients:

- 1 cup **shiroan (white bean paste)**
- 1/4 cup **mochi flour (shiratamako)**
- 1/2 cup **water**
- **Food coloring (optional)**

Instructions:

1. Cook shiratamako and water until thick.
2. Knead into shiroan and color as desired.
3. Shape into seasonal flower or nature-inspired designs.

Suama (Red and White Rice Cake)

Ingredients:

- 1 cup **joshinko (non-glutinous rice flour)**
- 1/2 cup **sugar**
- 1/2 cup **hot water**
- **Red food coloring**

Instructions:

1. Mix joshinko, sugar, and hot water until smooth.
2. Divide in half, dye one red.
3. Roll both into logs and twist them together.
4. Let cool before slicing.

Karinto (Sweet Fried Dough Sticks)

Ingredients:

- 1 cup **flour**
- 1 tbsp **brown sugar**
- 1/2 tsp **baking powder**
- 2 tbsp **water**
- **Oil for frying**
- **Honey or brown sugar syrup for coating**

Instructions:

1. Mix flour, brown sugar, baking powder, and water into a dough.
2. Roll into thin sticks and deep-fry until golden.
3. Coat with honey or brown sugar syrup.

Higashi (Pressed Dry Wagashi)

Ingredients:

- 1 cup **wasanbon sugar (or fine powdered sugar)**
- 1 tbsp **starch syrup or a few drops of water**
- **Food coloring (optional)**

Instructions:

1. Mix sugar with starch syrup to form a slightly damp powder.
2. Press into small wooden molds and carefully remove.
3. Let dry until firm.

Baked Sweet Potato (Yaki Imo)

Ingredients:

- 2 **Japanese sweet potatoes (Satsumaimo)**

Instructions:

1. Wash sweet potatoes and bake at 375°F (190°C) for 45–60 minutes.
2. Serve hot, optionally wrapped in foil for a traditional touch.

Japanese Parfait

Ingredients:

- 1 scoop **matcha or vanilla ice cream**
- 1/4 cup **sweet red bean paste (anko)**
- 1/4 cup **mochi pieces or dango**
- 1/4 cup **cornflakes or granola**
- **Whipped cream, fruits, and matcha jelly for topping**

Instructions:

1. Layer granola, anko, and ice cream in a tall glass.
2. Add whipped cream, mochi, and fruit.
3. Serve immediately.

www.ingramcontent.com/pod-product-compliance
Lightning Source LLC
LaVergne TN
LVHW081329060526
838201LV00055B/2538